EVENING
CLEARING

Poems and Drawings
from the Mountain

by
SHOZO KAJIMA

Translated by
GLENN GLASOW
and
YOSHIKO KAKUDO

Poems and Drawings by Shozo Kajima
Translated by Glenn Glasow and Yoshiko Kakudo

Executive Editor/Seiji Horibuchi
Editor/Yuki Inoue
Book Design/Shinji Horibuchi
Publisher/Keizo Inoue

Printed in Japan by Yokohama Taikido Inc.

This volume is a newly edited English edition of BANSEI,
originally published in 1985 by Shicho-sha in Tokyo, Japan.

ISBN1-56931-018-1   First Printing,1994

Cadence Books
A Division of Viz Communications, Inc.
P.O. Box 77010
San Francisco, California 94107

The verse on page 9
is quoted from
The Poetry of Li Shang-yin
by James J. Y. Liu.

CONTENTS

ひぐらし
蝉の合唱が
ステレオとなって
夕燕の反転する空に
ゆらめきながら昇ってゆく

晩晴第十歌

平成初年十一月
於大徳原梧室荘

EVENING CLEARING

Poems and Drawings
from the Mountain

by
SHOZO KAJIMA

Translated by
GLENN GLASOW
and
YOSHIKO KAKUDO

Cadence Books
San Francisco

天意憐幽草人間重晚晴

李嵐山
祥造書

Heaven seems to pity the sequestered blade of grass;
In the human world, we must treasure this evening clearing.

That professor who comes to stay
In the mountain cottage...
He's an odd one.

Yesterday I stopped, called and called.
No answer.
Went around to the back yard. There he squatted,
Sketching bamboo shoots.
Tapped him on the shoulder.
He turned, startled.
Then, of all things, he took something
Out of his ears.

"What are they?"
  "Ear plugs. A French invention. They expand
   In the ear to shut out all sound."
"But how then can you hear the birds, the streams,
 The wind in the bamboo?"

"Oh, I hear them...morning and evening.
　But during the day
　There is something I don't want to hear."
"What?"
　"Cars. When I hear them down there
　I start to wonder,
　Leave my books, my sketching.
　Sometimes I go down to the lower yard
　Just to look.
　It's not that I wait for visitors.
　It's only when I think I hear them
　I can't work."

So here he wears ear plugs.
But he looked so happy to see me
And offered me a cup of tea.

He's an odd one, eh?
That professor.

四月が過ぎて
咲かれた花ばかり
眺めていたが
やっと山里にも
遅い木々芽吹き
根雪よどけて
のだが
残がんだ
二二方
桜が咲いていたのか

I

Stung by insects in the field
I returned and opened the medicine chest.
There, poised imperiously,
A large aggressive
Black ant, antennae waving.
My amusement grew as I spoke to him.

    What do you want here?
    You...who have none of our
    Civilized maladies...what is
    This stale medicine to you?
    Your sharp sense of smell...
    Has it failed you?

Then, looking again at the
Black ant, I wondered.

Here...you in this medicine chest,
I in these mountains.
Have we both crawled into
Places we do not belong?
Is that what you tell me with
Proud antennae waving?

II

While here in the mountains
One acts in unexpected ways.

One summer evening
After the rainy season
On a forest path
I suddenly began to walk very slowly,
Slower than the dreamer Rosei
Approaching the Noh stage,
Step by step,
Feeling every shift of my body as I walked.

Why?
These legs which have obeyed
My every intention as I
Hurried through fifty years,
Now, rebellious, independent,

Have come into their own,
Walking their way.
Here in the mountains
Sometimes I let my body act
Outside the mind's desire.

Surrendering to my leg's independence
I moved very slowly.
Suddenly, more surprised than curious,
I began to see those smaller parts of Nature
Which escape the casual eye.
First, delicate wild orchids,
Then, the smallest pale blossoms,
Emerging from the forest, at the edge of the field
Scattered flakes of tomato blossoms,
Tiny purple lettuce flowers,
In each miniature
The full artistry of Heaven.

While admiring the delicate wax design
Of the snakewhip

My legs stopped. I turned.
There, the large orange
Trumpet blossoms of the pumpkin!
Their dramatic size shocked
My legs back to their normal gait.

Crossing the pasture, ascending the hill
I saw my cottage in the bamboo grove.
Those pink things under the eaves,
What are they?
Mere reflections of the
Red sky above the mountain?
Arriving, I looked closely to discover the
Delicate fans of silk tree blossoms.
Could such beauty be
Blessed with fragrance?
Instinctively I pulled the
Delicate, deep scarlet blossoms to my face.
At that moment, from the southern grove,
Cries from a summer cicada...only twice.
The fragile thread of the blossoms

Trembled slightly.
Astonished by this
Natural resonance I
Released the branch and
Turned toward my cottage.

Later that night while in the bath
A waka came to me.

      As night approaches,
      Their leaves closing in sleep,
      The cry of the evening cicada
      Gently sways
      The silk tree blossoms.

At that moment I laughed,
More in sadness than in joy, for
Here, alone, surrounded by the
Growing coolness of the evening
Whom would I sway,
With my poem, with my laughter?

そんな仕事のあと、私は雲仙の山波を眺める
その前山から庭に向けて、灰色の断雲が北へ動いて
ゆき、音が遠ざかる。あたりには夏の名残りの
積雲が立っている。はるか遠空近くは
秋の先がすでにきざしている。私は眼を戻して
松の梢に群がるつぼ花とみ見ると
オミナエシの黄の花冠と見える
二人には静かな死があるが
それは稲が先生に
じかに通じているのだ
それをその関係を
虫たちはよく知っているか
私たちは
こんな秋の光にかげる

晩晴太田歌
秋の海より

III

Staying here I find the empty shells of insects.
    (I killed some of them.)
This morning a black cricket lay dying on the porch,
Its legs trembling.
Tonight a tiny spider floated in my bath, unlamented.

Staying here I see drying grass and bushes.
    (I cut some of them.)
Five months ago I felled a tall acacia.
New shoots appeared.
Yesterday they were cut down with the autumn grass.
    (No police stopped my wildly swinging blade.)
The work finished, I gazed at the eastern range.
Before the peaks gray clouds moved,
Beyond, remnants of summer cumuli.
And streaming from the distant blue above
Covering all below,

An autumn light.
In the pines above spiders spun their web.
At my feet were late summer yellow blossoms.

Here death follows life,
An unbroken course
Silently understood by all.
But to us, without that autumn light...

This light from the vast sky
Reaches that city more removed from me
Than the clouds beyond the mountains.
There in the city a man falls:
The white ambulance,
The white hospital.
Away from this light
The intervening hands and instruments,
The artificial dusk.
And by that intervention understanding fades,
Something important is lost.

But staying here it can be seen,
However faintly, in the dry grass and insects.
Even by casual eyes, though faintly,
That Something shown by autumn light.

IV

Mornings are always the same:
        Rise, wash, sweep, dust,
        Fill the kettle,
        Turn on the propane
        And watch the heating water.

"A watched pot never boils."
        If true, I tell myself,
        Don't watch. Sit quietly.
        Look deep within yourself.
        But I find I am back staring
        At the water and reflected light.

Yes, it is that first light I see
Reflected, the faint rays
Of the morning sun
Streaming from the mountain top

Across the river
Through the red pine grove
Warming the throat of the waking bird,
Through my window,
Now reflected on the surface of the water.

Steam rises.
The light dims.
On the bottom of the pot single bubbles appear,
Swell, quiver and detach themselves.
(An ancient poet called these crab eyes.)
Slowly their number grows.
Three or four together
Sway in their ascent
To the surface
Where they stare upward.
(He called these fish eyes
And heard in the simmering water
The rain on pine branches.)
But modern heat is cruel.
The fish eyes soon
Rush to the surface,

Right and left,
Bumping, crashing, bursting.

I turn off the gas.
Steam gushes out
And the fish eyes retreat from the surface.
Slowly, little by little,
The light returnes and I hear the bird's song.

But wait.
Not yet.
Hold the bamboo dipper.
Gentle tea leaves
Cannot bear such heat.
Think of something...of her, so far away.
If I cannot wait for this
How can I be patient in the future?

But I find I cannot wait.
I pour the water, still too hot.
On the delicate leaves
And brew my bitter tea.

V

One evening, with the last brush stroke,
The pumpkin seemed to leap from its place on the table
Onto the white expanse of paper before me.
In the space around it
I wrote the waka
Grown slowly inside of me
Through all those ruined sketches.

> Doomed to be my
> Solitary evening repast,
> So peacefully
> The pumpkin waits.

My calligraphy became aggressive.
(My unbearable loneliness perhaps?)
One bold stroke flew over the paper
Threatening the pumpkin

Like the blade of a knife.
But finally,
"Done just right!" I said,
Rose quickly from my knees,
Kicked my ink and splattered
It across
The entire work.

More nights I sketched
And in this time
My loneliness eased, but so too
The calm grace of the pumpkin and
The strength of my calligraphy
Were lost.

One afternoon I took the pumpkin
To the kitchen,
Cut it,
Placed it in a pot,
Carefully balanced soy sauce, rice wine,
Simmered it slowly

猫り尾の

シ飴のために

割られたこて

まず眺むれば

貝若に
たろ
かな

And sat down alone to eat it.

The first taste,
Only a small piece, tentatively.
The delicate meat of the pumpkin,
The sweetness, saltiness, all mingled:
"Done just right!"
And I remembered that evening: the
Completed sketch, my joy, those same words.

But now I sat quietly
Eating, laughing, thinking:
The fragrance of the food,
The memory of those early sketches.

Yes,
Whatever I may have thought then
The one before me now
Is the real pumpkin
Done just right.

VI

Slowly, uphill,
On narrowing path,
Two men follow the Nakatagiri river.
High above the dam they stop
To sit on a white boulder in the stream.
Below, the valley in full fall color.
Beyond view, the Tenryu river.
Early snow swirls on
The peaks of Mount Senjo.

They sit for awhile
In silence.
One...bald, with high blood pressure,
Cannot know what his companion thinks,
What those narrow blood-shot eyes really see.
Nor can the other ...white hair, myopic,
With low blood pressure,

Know his friend's thoughts.

They munch rice balls,
Drink water from the stream.
    "Great view there..."
    "Wonderful water here..."
Here, where nature overwhelms
Eloquence falters.
Such cliches suffice.
Here, time is measured
By wind and shadow.

Over the larch forest shadows deepen.
From the valley, suddenly
Through the corridors of purple and red
A cold wind blows
Chilling their backs.

Soon the two men
Like birds on a branch will
Rise together,

Stand awhile, then leave.
But for a moment they sit,
Still gazing down.
This silent understanding
Shared by two
Who have ignored the glaring
Eyes of wives to come here
From the noise and grime of the world beyond.

VII

The morning song of the small bird,
Why does it sound so cheerful?
Why does the repeated phrase
Reverberate in endless changes?

    I wish my song to be that way,
    Joyous, from my heart.
    But I fear, I know
    That no one hears it.

With faith unquestioned
At the first warmth of the morning sun
He summons her
While perched on the highest branch
His beak a V, opened in song,
His tiny body becomes his voice
Calling to his mate.

As I sing at dusk
My song dies unheard,
My voice like the sighing wind
In the fog dampened grass of the valley.

But we share, this bird and I,
Our love of the forest
And our singing to our mates
To come to us.

VIII

In the chill
Dead of the spring night
I suddenly awoke.
Most of the time I fall asleep again,
But last night I lie there, thinking.

My long past
Of tepid anguish,
My short, uncertain future.
The flabbiness of my belly—
The toxic accumulation of emotion?
The fat of insensitivity—
Failure to exercise
Human feeling all those years?

This ominous ringing
In my ears, through my brain,

As I clung to things,
To selfish desires. Yes,
I began to hear it near the end
Of my prime of life.

I remember. I began to wear glasses
To appear intellectual
When I went abroad to study
Five years after the war.
The war.
It was then these hard lines of determination
Formed around my mouth
After being struck by a young officer.
His face I still remember,
His name, no longer.

But long before that I
Stopped hearing cries of the heart.
When that young girl called for help
As I stood on the bridge
I could hear only

My own selfish voice.

Already in my early childhood,
My taste dulled
By sweet indulgence,
My tiny nose already closed
To any fragrance
Beyond that crowded city,
I snuggled against my grandmother
Falling back to sleep.

A spring morning.
In the city already
Cherry trees bloom
In the haze of auto exhaust.
But here it is still early spring.
Shovel in hand
I go to dig radishes
Behind my cottage.
At the end of the garden
Two plum trees stand

Like an old peasant couple.
From their dark branches
Something shines in the morning light—
The first blossoms!
I leave my work to go and
Stand under the trees.

On the green branches
Are many black buds,
Only a few blossoms.
How white they are!
As white as the distant
Snowy peaks
But more brilliant than
The morning sun
Reflected there.

I stand
Between blossoms and snowy peaks
Remembering my thoughts of last night—
  When?

Where?
Who?
One by one,
How did those delicate blossoms
Of feeling fall from my boughs?

But now I shake my head.
It is spring,
The time for new blossoms.
And now it is morning
When night thoughts disperse.
Staring at the deep azure sky,
My cheek caresses
An open blossom.
As if brushing my face
A waka
Passes though my mind.

With the scent of
This blossom,
A visit to that

Old home
Deep in my memory.

A mediocre poem, I know,
But for a moment
The emptiness of this
Cold life is forgotten.

春過夏猶清

IX

This place—
On its southside the deep valley
With its forests of pine and larch trees,
The forest path upstream
Westward higher to the river-head
The small waterfall above
The large white rock in the clear stream—
All seems made for the poet.

But it was not poetry
I longed for that evening
As I entered the forest,
Turned left downstream toward the village,
Head thrust forward, walking fast.

From the valley to the red pine forest

The evening sun enveloped all
Casting slanted rays of gold
On ocher trunks where
Red and gold diffused to a
Radiance as if from the Western Pure Land—
An unworldly beauty.

Absorbed as I was in worldly thoughts
The sight did not delay me.
I kept my pace, descended
Past the larches to enter another
Red pine forest where I
Stopped suddenly, showered with the
Sad song of kanakana cicadas which
Filled the air, dripping from every branch,
Until the red and gold Pure Land
Seemed to tremble with snobbing—
A lament for the fleeting world.
I stood, transfixed and drenched
With the ceaseless shower of sound,
A waka welling up inside me.

At the edge of a field
The echoes of forest cicadas.
Shining only on that sound
The evening sun.

Leave off such thoughts,
I told myself,
Dinner and friends wait for you.

In long strides I crossed the meadow
Around the rice field
Then looked back.
There, above the forest, a wonderous sight!
The song of the cicadas seemed transformed into
Pure Spirit which rose toward the sky
Where evening swallows soared.

But I turned away onto
The asphalt road.
Rather the warmth of a bowl of rice, I thought,
Than the coolness of Pure Spirit.

Spiritual things are not for dinner conversation.
Better to pick some lilies for the table.
My eyes on the roadside
I hurried toward the darkening village.

X

The wind from the valley
Was strong and cold.
A black Siberian kite
Soared bravely above.
I was at the highest cable car station.
Borne toward the black peaks
By the cruel wind
The bird overhead
Made me think of the wife I left.

People told me she had gone
To a temple in the north
After she knew I had left her.
What was she seeking?
Like that bird that rides
The wind toward the cold mountain peaks,
What did she seek there?

Looking back down the valley
Beyond the yellowing larch forest,
Beyond the hills and fields
The bright sunlight on the
Bundles of rice straw
Reminded me of that one
Who, with the audacity of her
Young love, warmed my frozen heart
As if to bring forth
What was still alive in me.

The small iron cage arrived.
I was the only passenger.

There, hanging from a single thin cable,
Blown by the icy wind,
The dark peaks above,
The yellow fields below—
What is my karma?
I do not know.

But for the moment I believe this cable
Will not break.

The black kite soars
Behind me as I descend
Toward the shining fields.

たしかいたとえば師走の二十二日

冬至の日にここで独居するのな

変人のすることかもしれん

朝の七時もがと
なってようやく

東の遠い
山並が
とき色になる

午后に提案家や
柿枝を焼く

その煙に眼も
しばだくよう

遠い西山の枝鹿から夕間が漂いて
林はまやくも
夜写業を寒い気分を味き

九の前に多新は黒いな人でしかない

里小人ヨリ
詩書画拝

XI

Here alone...in itself no joy,
But the sharpened sense of life which
Solitude brings...
That is joyous.
Here with another...would that sense be shared?
With three of us...would two resent
My happiness?
So I am here alone.

Eccentric perhaps
To be here alone in the mountains
On this cold day,
The day of the winter solstice.
The sun waited until seven o'clock
To bathe the distant hills
In its soft pink glow.

After burning brush and leaves in the afternoon
Smoke-teary eyes watched the evening quickly
Creep from the valley to the fields to the hills
Until the forest breathed darkness and cold.
I stood, a shadowy midget,
Watching that evening light,
The orange glow, the golden
Rays from purple clouds
Reflected from snowy peaks and from
Something deep inside of me.
Cherishing the glow within, I
returned to the cottage.

What shall I eat tonight?
Ground meat from yesterday,
Some tofu.

After that spare supper
I passed the night
With a book of Tessai's paintings.
One bore a short poem.

I am here
In the mountains
For my love
Of the quiet.

Yes, that is it! I thought,
Not escape, not dull idleness,
But the full consciousness of being alive.

Eccentric, perhaps
Some city people say. Or might
They ask what secret grief
Or guilt or heinous crime
Has driven him to this dark place
On this long winter night?

XII

Last night, my heart trembling with joy,
I could not sketch.
Tonight only my hands tremble.
I keep drawing two blue irises,
The same flowers
They picked on the river bank.
Yesterday they came
With Lucky the cat.
The loneliness was lifted
And the entire cottage
Breathed with life.

I sketch in my six-tatami room.
She cooks our dinner as
She pages through an American magazine.
Curled in the rocking chair, her daughter
Is absorbed in the sequel to "The Jilted Maiden."

Here, in this small cottage
On the edge of the forest
In the glow of the moment's light
Our pasts are forgotten.

But Lucky has no past.
She walks the darkness alone.

The winds are quiet,
The forest still.
Then, a faint "meouw."
In the grass her
Shining yellow eyes approach.
Under the eaves she cries again
And the daughter lets her in.
"Don't fear," Lucky reassures her,
"Here the darkness has no scent of the past."

She hugs the cat.
Her mother unrolls our futons.
Unlocking the front door

I walk outside.
Suspended above,
The Milky Way—
Vast, uncharted,
Like the sea we sail in our love.
Love...an adventure, I know,
But never have I sailed
Such vastness
In such a frail craft!

XIII

Between the mulberry field and elm grove
The setting sun.
Would you say
My days too, are ending?
But wait, look,
There in the sky,
Still an evening glow!

How like my own, the thoughts
In these closing lines of
"A Response to Po-Chu-I on His Aging" by
The Tang Dynasty poet Liu-Yu.

Today I felt so keenly
The presence of this man
Who lived a thousand years before me.
His spirit seemed to hover over my cottage,

Embracing the dark peaks from
Kiso Koma mountain to Utsugi.

I went to pick some wild flowers.
Returning on the darkening path
I looked up at the sky and told myself
Yes, still
There is,
For me, too.

XIV

1

After sunset on a long summer day
I turn on all the lights
In the hall, the dining room,
In the six-tatami rooms in the north and west.
Even the lights in the bathroom and toilet.
A man must indulge one luxury
And brightening the night in this lonely cottage
Is my only indulgence.

As always, dinner was simple:
Cooked meat and tomatoes,
Cold tofu and miso soup.
After dinner
As I studied Tessai's sketchbook,
I was caught by an inscription

Which I copied in my notebook.

Accepting the
Simple country life,
What riches
Of the spirit.

On the garden side door
A soft tapping sound.
Alone in a mountain cottage
Such things startle.
Hurrying to the door
I saw in the glass
A thin bearded man
Staring at me,
Then realized it was
My own reflection.

In the window above the door
Dressed in gold vest with the
Finery of a 19th century dandy was

A large, brightly patterned moth.
Daytimes I welcome visitors,
Any dragonfly or butterfly,
But it is night so I ask
"What do you want?
Your simple country life...
What more riches do you seek?"
Wings flutter.
Gold powder dusts the window glass.
I laugh
And return to Tessai's sketchbook.

2

In autumn when
I extend my walks to the apple orchard
The mountain shadows fall suddenly.
The cottage and bamboo grove
Are dark when I return.
Often I have come to fill long evenings

With my favorite sounds as well as light.
That evening "The Marriage of Figaro"
Blared through the rooms as I scrubbed a pot.
Then, suddenly
I understood
That dandy who visited me that night.
Of course, he missed the long summer daylight
And flew from the dark forest
To knock on my door,
To share the bright inside.

Not so strange.
During those dark years
I too, dressed up every night to
Wander about in search of bright lights
Until I found that small intense light of love.
I thought I heard her ask,
"Is that why you are so contented now,
 Alone in the engulfing night?"

Through the small kitchen window

I saw the harvest moon
Rising over the eastern range,
Dispelling the darkness.

Suddenly I shook the water from my hands
And decided I would return tomorrow,
Through the valley,
Across the country
To the city,
To the brightly lighted
Houses, streets and hills,
To her.

Remember,
You should not leave
this earth unless
You've made it
a little lovelier.

B.S.R.

XV

How joyous that
Meeting at twilight
In Yokohama!
We walked slowly,
Watching the orange city lights
Reflected in the harbor.
A ship was leaving.
We called it our ship
And talked of sailing out into the world.

Inside, a voice asked me,
If there were such a time
Would I really
Board that ship?
Once aboard,
Would my heart still
Be in the mountains?

Here it is deep summer.
She will come soon,
Across the country
Up the valley
From the city,
Wearing her broad brim summer hat.
And after the joy of meeting again
We will watch the twinkling village lights,
Sitting, our hands in each other's lap,
Discussing the watermelons and tomatoes,
Waiting for the moon to rise over the mountains.

Could she live here
In this cottage?
If she were here
Would she still long for the sea?

> *There is only the joy of*
> *Viewing the mountain.*

Tessai wrote that when seventy-seven years old.

But someone half that age
Would long for the sea.

Still, there must be
A natural rhythm of things.
While I watch the seasons change on the mountain
She could sail the sea,
Both of us in that
Larger rhythm of love.
I hope I could be waiting
Like that mountain,
For autumn,
For the snow which follows.

XVI

Now apart from families
Two men sit
Silently eating.
Outside the brilliant sun
Of the usual late mountain spring which
Arrived even later this year.
Perhaps that is why
The forest and fields
Are so filled with warm light.
"My first taste of these.
  Wild aren't they? What are they?"
"Kogomi. Too hard?"
"No. All my teeth
  Are false, you know."

They walk a forest path.
The red buds are swelling

In the filtered sunlight.
From the valley below comes
The sound of rushing water.
    "Becoming a recluse...impossible for us!
    Much less the life of a sage."
        "I know. The Chinese poet-recluse
        Had family, house, farm,
        A leisurely country life."
    "For us now...
    Far beyond our means!"

They leave the forest to stand in a field.
A shimmering haze
Covers the Tenryu river.
Over the pink hue of budding mountain trees
Hangs a faint mist.
The snowy peaks from Senjo to Shiomi are about
To fly away into the deep blue
Where lonely, single
Clouds float.
    "Confronting the beauty of nature

Old age laments."
　　"Who are you quoting?"
"Yuan Chen, in a poem to Pao Cu-i."
　　"How old was he then?"
"O, perhaps our age."
　　"But for us, such aging...
　　We can't afford that yet."

Already sixty years old
Two men stand
Facing the beauty of spring
Without the freedom to lament.

雨の降りきる巻町を走ってきたが
これも畑に煙こそ片
志連此から谷や林も
雲霞に閉ざされている
私の心も悲しみに閉ざされたまゝ
雲の峯でい窿の下を
押しあけた

晴れ晴水雨気

XVII

Leaving the steady rain in Yokohama
I returned to find
Mountain, valley and forest
Shrouded in a heavy mist.
The same heaviness lay on my heart
As I pushed open the cottage door.

My eyes fell first on the
Old chipped Korean bottle
Which still held the stem of plum blossoms
Placed there last spring,
(I sketched it one day)
Now dried, dark,
The petals fallen...
An image of my own heart.
I stood there staring,
Holding my bag.

That was yesterday.
Today in brighter moments
I sat on the terrace to sketch the
Western peaks which seemed to
Move in and out of the mist
From my notebook I took these
Lines by Yuan Mei
To inscribe my sketch.

> *Now clear, now raining*
> *The path dry, now wet.*
> *Mountains overlapping*
> *Half light, half shadow.*

Lifting my brush from these lines
All pretense faded: I could not
Live as a recluse poet.
In the setting sun
The yard before the cottage
Filled me with sadness.
On the grass, here and there,

Mounds of red clay dug up by moles,
A tangled mass of weeds
And dried vines,
The pine seedling I planted
Now bent and dying,
Debris and neglect...
So much like my inner life.

From the bamboo grove below
A lone bird
Flew over the garden into the forest,
Darted among the trees and
Disappeared in the darkness:
That love which fled from me.
From the depths of the forest a
Single call to her.

遠いものが
いつやら遠く
十二月の
透明な光のなかに
消えてゆく

鳥の影
三好豊一郎

XVIII

Alone under the lamp,
When I finished reading
Your new book of poems
I noticed the scattered sounds of rain drops.
I arose and walked out onto the terrace.
Night fog filled the forest
Leaving only tree tops visible.
From below, the sound of the
Raging stream turning stone on stone.
Listening to it,
Inside of me, the disquieting wish
To ask you about those poems,
The heavy shadow hanging over them.
Your letter mentions being ill.
Truly an illness of body?
Or of spirit, crushed by the
Weight of city life?

Only four years ago
One clear August day
We walked through the forest
Along the valley deep into the mountains
To sit on a white boulder,
Viewing the Tenryu valley.
It was there we ate our rice balls.
Who was first? Perhaps it was together that we
Jumped naked into the pure mountain water,
Bathing, splashing, shivering and laughing.

That was only four years ago,
Yet now from the noisy city
You write of being ill and say
You cannot visit me this summer.
I sit here saddened
That your poems
No longer hold that vibrant happiness.

After a long separation
The Sung poet Ouyang Shiu

Wrote a poem to his older friend Mei Yaochen.

When you say you are aging
I cannot hold my tears.
Though younger than you, with
My white hair, I too, feel age.

How like those poets
Of the distant past we are!
And so, I wish to send
Those encouraging words
The younger poet wrote in other lines.

Who pronounces you old?
Your poems still show
A ruggedness and strength.

Yes, we are bent
By the weight of
The last four years,
But we know our poems are unbroken.

But it is time for us
To leave the pleasures of the seaside
For the quiet of the mountains,
The bright summer for that
Season best for us.

I ask again,
If not this summer
Can we
One day in late autumn
Walk together again
Through the golden forest of larch trees
Along this valley?

XIX

The snow which fell on the shortest day
Remained all winter.

On Christmas day I sat
Facing the yard.
Snow covered the dried grass and fields
Down to the edge of the dark forest.
There, in a shiny strip of white,
A single sumac tree,
A red torch against the brilliant whiteness.

From the book on my knees
I read Li-he's poem "Grieving for a Dead Mistress,"
Re-read the poem, feeling its rhythm.
Again I stared at the snow forest,
Then read the poem again.
The two hundred years separating Li-he from me

雪は庭の芝生にひろがり
枯草の間でわずかに光り
黒い林の根方で消えていた
そこに一本
紅葉したぬるでが残っていた

Slowly faded. I began to respond to his poem,
Line by line.

Those seven years, a short dream
        For us, a shorter dream.
So painfully clear in memories.
        The distant forest blurs
        As I remember.
Holding her brush, she called herself my student.
        She too, came as my student.
        In the end I loved her.
Like an angel she attended me, the sick Yuima.
        She encouraged, cared for,
        Sometimes loved this tired old man.
Her shadow on the screen, hair in disarray.
        Ah, Li-he, for me too
        Memories of joyous nights!
Her trailing sleeves blown by the breeze.
        We too, walked that forest path
        But now
Today, vainly searching for a trace of her

I cannot stop
       She has gone
       To seek another teacher.
My hair from growing white.
       I found that love
       When my hair was already white.

I turn to gaze at the snow.
The forest, the
Lone flaming sumac tree.

XX

Already spring, yet
With this cold inside my chest and
The cold outside, the overcast sky,
A dreary day.

A white flake flickered by my window.
And another. What is this?
I cursed. Snow again!
So late in March?

Bringing in the mat from the terrace I saw
Low clouds over the forest but
No snow falling. Yet
Another white flake, not snow, but
Blown by the wind,
A petal from a plum tree.

I placed a blossoming branch in the
Old Korean bottle. Then,
Thinking of my failure last year,
I spread the Chinese paper and
Began drawing, very carefully.
Still unable to capture
The fragrance of the plum on paper.
Again and again I tried, until dusk.

Looking up, startled, I saw
Heavy snow outside, falling everywhere
Covering the forest.
        Ah yes, I know...
        Spring in the mountains.

I cooked my evening food, ate,
And heated my bath.

Suddenly in the bath a
Waka came to mind.
Dripping I rushed to my painting and

In characters as small as the buds
On the branches I wrote,

    As falling snow grows heavier
    With the gathering dusk,
    The spring fragrance grows stronger.
    All eludes
    My faltering brush on paper.

A poem too delicate
For my crude painting,
But perhaps between the two, a balance.
I put down my brush,
Laughed, and shivering
Returned to the warm bath.

The Path

In the present
No tears
      Only those welling up from the past
Or fears
      Only those which fall from thoughts of the future

In the present
Pulsating life we know
That first love...passion
      Only to learn that it too, will pass

You have reached the time
I tell myself
When you wish to climb the mountain
To feel the cool white snow,
There to seek that
Second love...compassion.

The path is there
In this present moment,
A path I must clear and
Clear again
On my way to that
Snow covered mountain.

LINES
IN THE DRAWINGS

Page 6

The song of the cicadas seemed transformed into/Pure Spirit which rose toward the sky/Where evening swallows soared. (IX)

Page 13

In the world of men it is summer now and the fragrance of the year past;/In this mountain-temple the peach-blossom has just reached its prime,/I have long wondered what becomes of Spring, and did not know where to look;/Now I know that when it leaves the plains it is here that Spring hides. (*Po Chu-i, trans. by Arthur Waley*)

Page 20

The work finished, I gazed at the eastern range./Before the peaks gray clouds moved,/Beyond, remnants of summer cumuli./And streaming from the distant blue above/Covering all below,/An autumn light./In the pines above spiders spun their web./At my feet were late summer yellow blossoms./Here death follows life,/An unbroken course/Silently understood by all./But to us, without that autumn light... (III)

Page 29

Doomed to be my/Solitary evening repast,/So peacefully/The pumpkin waits. (V)

Page 42

Spring is gone, but the summer air is still fresh. (*Li Shang-yin, trans. by James J. Y. Liu*)

Page 50

Eccentric perhaps/To be here alone in the mountains/On this cold day,/The day of the winter solstice./The sun waited until seven o'clock/To bathe the distant hills/In its soft pink glow./After burning brush and leaves in the after-noon/Smoke-teary eyes watched the evening quickly/Creep from the valley to the fields to the hills/Until the forest breathed darkness and cold.(XI)

Page 59

Passing a pass, we saw/Autumn festi-val, far down/in a village. (*S. Kajima's haiku*)

Page 72

Leaving the steady rain in Yokohama/I returned to find/Mountain, valley and forest/Shrouded in a heavy mist./The same heaviness lay on my heart/As I pushed open the cottage door. (XVII)

Page 76

A far one,/getting more so, into/the clear light of December. (*Toyoichiro Miyoshi, trans. by S. Kajima*)

Page 82

Snow covered the dried grass and fields/Down to the edge of the dark forest./There, in a shiny strip of white,/A single sumac tree,/A red torch against the brilliant whiteness. (XIX)

Page 91

A sketch of Kajima's atelier in Yokohama called Bansei-Kan.

Shozo Kajima

One of the meanings of the original title of this book, Bansei, is "a late bloomer." Born in 1923, Kajima himself was a late bloomer, both as an artist and as a poet. A former English professor and scholar of American literature, Kajima has translated a number of American novels into Japanese, including five major works by William Faulkner. He has also written several books on American literature. Kajima was sixty years old when he held his first one-man exhibition of sumi-e drawings in Tokyo. A year later, he published this book in Japan.

Kajima's most recent passion is the revival of the oriental art form known as sansui. Basically an expression of the Taoist world through a combination of illustration and verse, sansui means "mountain-water" and is traditionally displayed in either book or hanging scroll form. Kajima's interest in this ancient art form has helped to revive it in a modern context, as the tradition was virtually lost in Japan upon the death of the great sansui master Tessai Tomioka in 1923. Interestingly enough, this is also the same year in which Kajima was born.

Glenn Glasow

Was born in Minnesota in 1924. He now holds a position as Professor Emeritus in the Music and Asian Studies Department at the California State University in Hayward. Dr. Glasow has visited Japan twenty-one times since he first saw the country while on an international education grant in 1965. He has given lectures on contemporary music in Japan, both in public and private programs. He reports that his interest in traditional Japanese arts has influenced his work as a composer.

Yoshiko Kakudo

Was born and raised in Japan. After receiving a Master of Arts degree in 1964 from the University of California, Berkeley, she began her museum career as a curator of Japanese art. She is now a Curator Emeritus at the Asian Art Museum and pursues various creative activities in her free time.